HELPS FOR STUDENTS OF HISTORY SERIES 94

Oral History

Talking about the Past

Robert Perks
British Library National Sound Archive

Published by
The Historical Association in association with The Oral History Society
59a Kennington Park Road
London SE11 4JH

Acknowledgements

Front Cover: **A school pupil listens in to an oral history recording**

I would like to thank Paul Thompson with whom I co-wrote the booklet *Telling It How It Was* (BBC, 1989) from which I have drawn parts of this book. Alan Ward and staff at the National Sound Archive and the National Life Story Collection have once again provided advice and support, as have my fellow committee members of the Oral History Society. Clive Knowles has been a patient, understanding and interested editor. The photographs appear courtesy of the Bradford Heritage Recording Unit.

This pamphlet has been edited by
Clive H. Knowles

The Historical Association, founded in 1906, brings together people who share an interest in, and love for, the past. It aims to further the study and teaching of history at all levels: teacher and student, amateur and professional. This is one of over 100 publications available at very preferential rates to members.
Membership also includes journals at generous discounts and gives access to courses, conferences, tours and regional and local activities. Full details are available from The Secretary, The Historical Association, 59a Kennington Park Road, London SE11 4JH, telephone: 0171-735 3901.

The publication of a pamphlet by the Historical Association does not necessarily imply the Association's approval of the opinions expressed in it.

The Oral History Society encourages and supports the collection and study of people's unique personal memories through twice-yearly conferences, journals, publications and a regional network of representatives. Details from the Secretary, Sociology Department, Essex University, Colchester C04 3SQ.

Designed and prepared by Margaret Pierre

ISBN 0 85278 391 4 2nd revised edition
(ISBN 0 85278 343 4 1st edition)

Originated and published by The Historical Association, 59a Kennington Park Road, London SE11 4JH and printed in Great Britain by DS Redesign, 53 Jute Lane, Brimsdown, Enfield EN3 7JL.

Contents

Introduction:
What is Oral History?   5

The Origins of Oral History   8

Collecting Oral History   12
  Before the interview   12
  Equipment   14
  The interview   17
  After the interview   20

Using Oral History   26

Notes and References   33

Further Reading   37

Useful Contacts   42

Introduction: What is Oral History?

Oral history is spoken history: it is the recording of people's unique memories and life stories. Over the past thirty years talking directly to the makers of history has emerged not only as one way in which historians can discover more about the past, but also as an historical discipline in its own right.

At its best oral history can provide completely new information about whole areas of our past which is unavailable from written or printed sources. Even where documentary sources are available they are often uninformative or inaccessible, for example under the thirty-year rule for government papers. And for some topics, like personal and family relationships, written sources based on individual experience are almost entirely absent. An extract from an interview with a woman born in Barrow in 1904, from Elizabeth Roberts' *A Woman's Place*, illustrates the power of the spoken word to fill gaps in our understanding of the past:

Half past seven we had to be in. And when I was courting Reg, it was half past nine. We used to go into the parlour when Reg and I were courting and about half past nine they used to give Reg a cup of tea and m'dad would get the alarm clock off the mantelpiece and wind it, he was ready for bed and that was a good hint for Reg to go. He had to go then...They weren't terribly strict, but perhaps I think we obeyed them better than children do nowadays.[1]

This is hardly the kind of history that many people learnt at school but in providing new information it also adds a human context and recognises the value of individual experience so obviously missing from standard social histories. Oral history personalises, colours and enlivens. It rescues the individual from the crowd, and redresses a balance which has tended to give greater credence to the powerful and influential, 'the great and the good', in society, to the detriment of the ordinary and everyday. This is not, of course, to deny a role for oral history in studying group or class behaviour, or in 'elite' political, business or economic histories, where interviewing has proved to be a valuable tool in offering new insights into the interplay of personalities and events, and in some cases a valuable new factual record, as this extract from an interview with a Lloyds underwriter in the City of London reveals:

The job was purely a clerk. Nothing more, nothing less. A very junior clerk. It was very much a pen-pushing job, copying into ledgers, shuffling masses of bits of paper...I ran errands and they used to send me out into Leadenhall Market to get their cheese or their bacon or whatever. I was in charge of the arrival and the departure of the books, the ledgers. Of course Lloyds could have been destroyed or struck by bombs or by fire — all the underwriters' books were kept in the sub-basement of the building. My first duty was to go down in one of these old-fashioned gated lifts, down into the bowels of the building, down half-lit corridors into a dungeon-type room where there were rows and rows of porters' trolleys. On each of these trolleys was a pile of ledgers and one of those was mine.[2]

Oral history can also make us look afresh at assumptions we may have drawn from documentary sources or from hearsay, and encourage us to pay attention to marginalised groups in society, many of them previously hidden from history, for example women, gay people, people with disabilities, and ethnic groups. For the first time oral history has enabled the personal stories of immigrants to Britain to be heard, as this example from a man arriving from India in the 1960s testifies:

When I came my dream shattered the moment I got off the plane, you know. I saw the buildings — black, everywhere. I came in March and it was still wintry and it was so dark. You could see the pigeon droppings everywhere. I said 'My goodness, it's supposed to be a heavenly place!' And when I came I found out that everything was just the same as you find in India — mugging, cheating, telling lies...I was very depressed. I thought I'd see wonderful things. Even the Christmas cards we used to get from Britain were so beautiful.[3]

Oral history is the only type of history in which it is possible to question the makers of history face-to-face. One historian expressed his excitement at shaking the hand of the person who had shaken the hand of the Duke of Wellington, and there is something uncanny about interviewing, for example, someone in the 1980s like the late Benjamin Kagan. Born in 1878 in pre-Revolutionary Russia, Kagan was too old to be conscripted

for the First World War and only learnt to speak English when he fled to Britain in his fifties. At over one hundred years old his recall of his early life was remarkable.[4] Equally exciting is to hear someone speak about Victorian London's underworld, not from the viewpoint of a politician or a judge or a policeman (though that is rare enough), but from that of a criminal, as this extract shows:

I learnt pickpocketing from a chap I'd met in Wormwood Scrubs. His name was Edward Spencer...just like the Artful Dodger in Dickens. The other fellows were much older and took a real pride in their work. Spencer wouldn't let me go with him, but he told me how it was done and helped me practice. Women were the easiest to take from. They didn't have handbags then, but used to have pockets at the back of their skirts. It was easy to cut them away — they didn't even notice what had happened. Whoever invented these pockets must have been a whizzer. Wallets were more difficult because they were kept in breast pockets, and fly-shooting you had to be ready to run. Pickpocketing men and women were two completely different lines. The Jewish boys, down in Whitechapel, were very good whizzers, but they only went in for women. Spencer's lot only went for men, and One-eyed Charlie's gang were the same — though mostly he was a van-dragger — he wasn't a clever thief at all. Soon I had my own little team. Mostly we went pickpocketing about Whitechapel and Petticoat Lane, where the crowds were for the market...I was the gaffer. I looked after the others, always got them to do the pickpocketing. When they got it they would give it to me and I would do the selling and the sharing out of the proceeds.[5]

In schools oral history allows characters to jump from the page and in so doing brings history to life. It is an involving, demystifying and accessible history: anyone can pick up a tape recorder and talk to an older member of the family or a neighbour. It can also leap generation gaps and restore a sense of self-worth to older people who often feel their lives are of no interest, and who feel marginalised by society. But it is also an essential tool for a local historian to check written sources of the recent past and put flesh on the bare bones of history. There is a desperate need to collect interviews on a whole range of topics or we are in danger of losing a vast databank of individual memories which once gone are gone forever.

Collecting oral history is not always easy: people forget things, their memories play tricks by 'telescoping' events together or changing their order. They will occasionally subconsciously repress painful memories or artificially highlight their own role in a particular event. The dynamics and atmosphere of the interview situation itself may also influence what a person says: they might, for example, open up and empathise more with a man than a woman. But often the *way* of remembering something is as important as *what* is remembered, by giving us insights into how people interpret their own lives. The important point, of course, is that all historical sources, whether they are documentary or oral, are subject to the same influences of selectivity, interpretation and partiality. Each oral history interview is one individual piece of a complex jigsaw which, when assembled, gives us a clearer view of our past.

This pamphlet will explore the modern origins of oral history as an historical source; explain in detail how to go about collecting and organising it; and give some examples of how it has been used successfully in a wide range of different ways.

The Origins of Oral History

Although oral history is the newest form of history because it uses modern technology, the tape recorder, there is nothing new about talking to older people about the past, especially when written sources were absent or inadequate. Folk tales, myths and family histories have been passed down by word of mouth as long as human society has existed, [6] and even today in African tribal societies oral tradition retains a far more important role than written sources, as Alex Haley discovered in trying to trace his own family's roots in West Africa.[7] In Britain this kind of oral tradition remained predominant over written sources until relatively recently, and although nowadays more ephemeral audio-visual media (especially television) dominate our accumulation of information about the world, we still rely on the oral transmission of stories and experiences of family and friends to conduct our everyday lives. The passing down of childcare methods from mother to daughter is a case in point.

One of the first examples of oral history appears in the eighth century when the Venerable Bede, in compiling his *History of the English church and people*, based his description of Anglo-Saxon England at least partly on oral testimony: 'I am not dependent on any one author but on countless faithful witnesses who either know or remember the facts, apart from what I know myself'.[8] Although the arrival of printing did little to erode oral tradition in a largely illiterate society, it did begin the evolution of the respectability of the printed word which has so fixated generations of school pupils into thinking that the written word is the 'truth' and the spoken word is in some way suspect. Both, of course, are historical sources to be treated in the same way: as subjective and partial. In fact scholars in the eighteenth and early nineteenth century would have found the tendency by modern academics to dismiss oral sources as unsound. A.J.P. Taylor is famously quoted as saying that 'In this matter I am an almost total sceptic...Old men drooling about their youth: no',[9] yet Samuel Johnson noted in 1773 that 'You are to consider, all history was at first oral', and appealed for an oral history project on the 1745 Rebellion![10] And well-established nineteenth century historians such as Macaulay viewed reminiscences, oral traditions and folk tales as essential sources of equal merit to written sources.

It was not, however, until the mid-nineteenth century, with the emergence of the field-work method in social research, evident for example in Engels, *Condition of the working class in England in 1844*, Mayhew and Booth's studies of London and

Rowntree's study of York, that talking to people about their individual experiences gained some currency amongst social historians. The methods and intentions of these mainly middle class, philanthropic 'social explorers' varied considerably.

Most were to some extent influenced by the advent of the first census in 1801 and by Royal Commissions which frequently gathered evidence through interviews — sometimes moving personal testimonies — reproduced verbatim in their published reports. Charles Booth in his innovatory *Life and labour of the people of London*[11] was far from radical in his political views but was firmly committed to the 'objectivity' of scientific analysis. A similar approach characterised Lady Bell's study of Middlesbrough in *At the works* (1904) in which she used a questionnaire and a sample of 200 families. More polemic and impressionistic was Maud Pember Reeves, *Round about a pound a week* (1913), a study of women and poverty in south London.[12]

This use of individual oral testimony was not confined to social investigation: John Morley's *Life of William Ewart Gladstone* was based on conversations with the Liberal prime minister's contemporaries and friends.[13] In labour history, Sidney and Beatrice Webb undertook systematic oral history interviewing for their books, *The co-operative movement in Britain* (1891) and *History of trade unionism* (1894). And in 1906 leading economic historian J.H. Clapham called for the training of interviewers to collect the memories of businessmen as 'the best original authorities...with them die some of the most valuable records of nineteenth-century history'.[14]

By the inter-war period social investigation had become more respectable and a clutch of new studies such as the Pilgrim Trust's *Men without work* (1938) and A. Hutt's *The condition of the working class in Britain* (1933) used personal testimonies to highlight the poverty being caused by unprecedented levels of unemployment. At around the same time in the United States President Roosevelt's experimental New Deal Federal Writers' Project set out to conduct hundreds of life story interviews with agricultural workers, the unemployed, former slaves, Indians and many others.[15] It was one of the first attempts to bring anthropologists, sociologists and historians together and the first to attempt to make permanent the voices of their interviewees. Although Thomas Edison had invented the phonograph in 1877, partly as a means of recording his own family's history, early recording technology was not well suited to oral history fieldwork. By modern-day standards sound reproduction was poor and recordings lasted only a matter of minutes. Machines which cut the sound directly onto discs improved matters, and were used with some success by early anthropologists, but were cumbersome and expensive. It was only with the arrival of tape recorders around the time of the Second World War, followed in the sixties by compact audio cassettes, that it became possible to gather high quality oral history recordings in permanent form and make the notebook obsolete.

It was in the 1940s that the phrase 'oral history' itself is generally accepted to have been coined by American academic Allan Nevins, who began recording the memories of great men in American life.[16] Oral history blossomed in a society less hidebound by the conventions of document-based historical research, but the emphasis on elites was to remain prevalent in the States until the 1970s. This was in marked contrast to the British experience. Here, oral history's rise paralleled the post-war boom in social history and sociology, fostered by the founding of the new universities of the sixties. It was at one of these new universities, Essex, that a sociologist Paul Thompson initiated the first large-scale oral history programme in Britain in which 459 Edwardians, born between 1872 and 1906, were interviewed about their family and work experiences.[17]

At around the same time the History Workshop movement, with its interest in popular involvement in labour and feminist history, and the emergence of a new wave of working-class autobiographical and creative writing, all encouraged an atmosphere of shared personal expression and a desire to use new sources to redress the balance of history towards ordinary people. Added to this were changes in school history with a new emphasis on using original sources and in finding out, which stimulated oral history project work.[18] Growing numbers of local and family historians began to gather oral testimony from within their local communities, and libraries, museums and record offices came to realise the potential of oral recordings to fill in gaps in their book stock and artefact collections. In 1969 the Oral History Journal was created, followed in 1973 by the Oral History Society. Among its supporters was George Ewart Evans, whose innovative Suffolk interviews from the fifties onward had sought to capture a disappearing agricultural way-of-life and earned him the tag of 'father of oral history' in

Britain. He published extensively and the extract that follows is testimony to the enormous power of what he termed 'spoken history'. It is as much the *way* the story is related — the dialect words and the cadences of speech — which is remarkable, as the information about sheep-shearing before the First World War it contains:

You trimmed the sheep's body first, and you opened the front right up to the neck just as though you were unbuttoning a shart or a weskit. Then you cut down the back legs where the wool hangs over; and you did the same for the front. Leave it till later you wouldn't get at the wool that just lay there. Then you set the sheep on its backside and you clipped up one side, just over the backbone. You twizzled the sheep round and set into your work where you left off. Bellying — trimming the front — was the first job they gave the young 'colts', the beginners; and the old 'uns would have to finish off. Using the old hand-shears you had to hev a platform. If you hadn't a board, you couldn't set the heel o' your shears down: it would cetch in the ground. It's different with machine-shears: you can clip a sheep on the ground quite easily with them.[19]

The popularity of Evans's books, and of Ronald Blythe's *Akenfield: portrait of an English village* (1969), showed the tremendous potential for oral history at a time when people such as Charles Parker and Ewan MacColl were forging a new form of radio, the *Radio Ballads*, which offered uninterrupted airtime for ordinary people's life stories to be heard in their own words. *The Long March of Everyman* followed in 1971, comprising interviews with 800 people from all over Britain, and established the BBC Sound Archive as a major source of oral history recordings in its own right.

Documentary photographers, like the inner-city Survival Programmes project, began to use interviews to complement images and television was popularising personal histories through such series as Stephen Peet's *Yesterday's Witness*,[20] the predecessor of Television History Workshop's later work, and other oral history-based series such as *All Our Working Lives, Out of the Doll's House, A Century of Childhood* and *A Secret World of Sex*.

By the 1980s hundreds of oral history groups and projects had sprung up all over Britain; some of them, as in Dundee, Bradford, Leicester and Southampton, evolving local sound archives containing many hundreds of interviews. Many were innovatory: the Hall-Carpenter Oral History Archive carried out extended oral history work with gay people; the Ethnic Communities Oral History Project with gypsies and travellers; the Bradford Heritage Recording Unit with Asian and East European migrants. Many involved people without formal historical training, who learned new skills. Some became involved in the emergence of reminiscence and life review 'therapy' with older people, as it was recognised that oral history could act as stimulus material to encourage older people to reminisce about the past as a means not only of entertainment but, with the confused elderly, of 'reality orientation'.[21] Social history museums greeted oral history, both as a means of getting in touch with their public and as a way of making displays relevant to local people.[22] At the British Library National Sound Archive the establishment of the National Life Story Collection, and the appointment of the first curator of oral history, provided a new national focus for oral history with a permanent institutional base. And with the role accorded oral history in the new National Curriculum for history in schools it has now arrived as a basic tool in our understanding of the past.[23]

Collecting Oral History

Before the interview

When first setting out to talk to people about the past it helps to be clear about what you hope to achieve. Oral history is suited to individuals working independently, or as part of a group. The main interest may be in historical research, or drama, or teaching children, or helping older people, or simply wanting to find out about the past. Different aims can be combined, but it is essential to decide which comes first.

It is helpful to select a theme. This could be recording a family history to complement other records, or an autobiography. A particular community could be chosen — a village, a neighbourhood, or a street or block of flats — in which the project could look at its recent history overall: changes in home life, work, leisure, religion, how the buildings and streets and open spaces were used. Or you could concentrate on a single theme: on childhood or youth or marriage; on a particular industry or factory; on entrepreneurs or trade unionists; on an ethnic group; on a particular voluntary society, church or chapel; on a political campaign; on women's history; on war or peacetime; on a type of leisure — dancing, whippet racing, polo, etc. Selecting a theme focuses the interview programme and keeps it manageable.

Background research is an essential first step before actually setting out with a tape recorder. Find out what documentary sources are available about the chosen topic (there may not be very much), and if there are old newspapers, or maps, or existing oral history collections which might help. Part of the importance of research is to find out as much as you can about the person you are going to see. If they are well-known or have written about themselves this will be relatively easy: you can read *Who's Who*, newspaper reports, biographies, previous interviews, company profiles and so on. If they are not, it is a good idea to read around what you know of them and their occupation, using perhaps local history books and more general books to give you a context. But over-preparation is possible. It is most important to get a clear framework in your head of what you want to ask.

It is one of the frequent criticisms of oral history that memory is fallible and can distort. We know that memory is selective: that it is shaped by conscious and unconscious suppression, and also by reinterpretation. Recent research of memory processes suggests that the most drastic selection takes place in the shaping and organising of memory immediately after an experience.[24] This applies to almost all

12

historical documentation. So oral history should be treated with the same rigour as any historical document. As countless court cases witness, there can be as much conflict of memory hours or days as years after an event. But as time goes on, memory is slowly eroded; and people also re-evaluate their earlier years: a phase of 'life review' in which their early memories become clearer, and also franker. Deliberate misinformation about the past is very rare.

Memory is a mixture of fact and opinion, and both are important. Individuals differ a lot in their range of detailed memory: some will be worth recording for many hours, others more briefly. All of them taken together gradually create a jigsaw of past experiences. Generally direct experience is much more trustworthy than indirect, so it is a good idea when interviewing to press people to give personal examples to back up generalised comments. Repeated patterns of everyday life are often better remembered than single events. Few people are good on dates, and it is very common to 'telescope' two similar events into a single memory. For example people who lived through both world wars have been known to get them mixed up.

An oral historian has to be sensitive to these characteristics of memory in deciding what to ask, how to balance the oral evidence against other sources, and how to make use of what is recorded. But it is equally important to recognise that the way in which people make sense of their lives is valuable historical evidence in itself.

Seeming irrelevancies such as false interpretations of the facts, rumours and gossip, unrealised hopes, suppressed desires: all contribute to the driving force of everyone; to our consciousness, individual and collective. Life story evidence is by its nature subjective. Each life is just one of many perspectives on the past. Using memory in this way is more difficult, but it is one of the unique opportunities in oral history work.

It also helps in deciding who to interview. Sometimes the choice is obvious from the topic itself. If you are recording your family, interview as many members as you can; or if you are reconstructing an event, or a campaign, or a society, search for all those still alive who played key roles. But for many topics, it is important that different perspectives should be represented , for example, women as well as men; people of different ages; different social classes in a community; different types of worker; different political opinions; both those who succeeded and those who failed.

Finding people to interview often concerns people initially but in fact it is rarely a problem. Appeals through newspapers, the local radio or perhaps an advert in a shop window are all worth trying. As are old people's day centres, homes, clubs, community groups, trade unions and local history societies. Sometimes social workers or doctors will make suggestions. And once the interviews start people will suggest colleagues, friends and neighbours. Many local history projects are frequently inundated with potential interviewees who they have difficulty finding time to interview.

The next stage is to compile an overall question plan. Opinions vary on how structured this should be. Some oral historians favour detailed questionnaires to enable careful cross checking and comparative analysis. Others believe that questionnaires can be too rigid and tend to cut off interesting but unforeseen avenues that emerge in the interview. On balance questionnaires are best used as memory joggers: having a clear chronological framework to guide the interview is more important. It is essential to give the interviewee plenty of time and space to tell you what they think matters.

The main rules in asking questions are: always keep them short, use plain words, and avoid suggesting the answers by asking leading questions. So rather than, 'Did you have a poor upbringing?' ask, 'Can you describe your childhood?' Some types of questions encourage precise answers: 'What did you do next?' Others are open, inviting descriptions, comments, opinions: 'Can you describe the room?' 'How did you feel about that?', 'Why did you do that?'

Leaving aside the type of questions there are some questions which should be asked in every interview: when and where the person you are recording was born, where they lived, what their parents did and what their own main jobs were. These are partly warm-up questions but they also provide essential information to place the whole interview in context. Some topics will need a very specialised and focused interview. And this also goes for some individual people. Generally, however, a life story or biographical approach is best in which an interviewee is encouraged to relate their life chronologically, beginning with family background, grandparents,

parents, and siblings (including topics such as discipline), then onto childhood home (housework, chores, mealtimes), leisure (street games, gangs, sport, clubs, books, weekends, holidays, festivals), politics and religion, schooling (key teachers, friends, favourite subjects), early relationships, working life (first job, a typical working day, promotion, pranks and initiation, trade unions and professional organisations), and finally later family life (marriage, divorce, children, homes, money, neighbours, social life, hopes). It can take anything from two to twenty-two hours to record a full life story depending on the individual's age, memory, stamina, breadth of experience and story-telling abilities.

Equipment

Getting the right tape recording equipment and knowing how to use it is an essential first step to preserving people's life stories on tape, whether it be audio tape or video tape. Each recording is a unique and irreplaceable historical 'document' which can be used in many different ways afterwards — perhaps on radio or television — so getting the best quality recording which reproduces the original as closely as possible is vital.

There are many different makes and models of portable audio tape recorders on the market but only three basic types: digital, reel-to-reel (or open reel) and cassette recorders. The professional high quality digital and reel-to-reel machines, which are used by broadcasters, give the best results and reel-to-reel tapes are generally regarded as better for archiving. But few people can afford these machines.

If you have £1000 or more to spend, then it is worth thinking about buying a Uher Report Monitor reel-to-reel recorder or a Sony Digital Audio Tape (DAT) recorder. However DAT tape is archivally unproven and should in due course be copied onto a more reliable digital medium for long-term storage. The same goes for many of the other newer digital formats like the DCC (Digital Compact Cassette) and the Mini-Disc (a small CD or Compact Disc). Nevertheless for museum gallery use digital sound is more versatile for a variety of 'visitor-friendly' playback purposes, for example by transfer to interactive touch-screen CD, and digital sound has the huge advantage that it can be copied or 'cloned' many times without loss of quality.[25]

For more modest budgets it is possible to buy an excellent portable cassette recorder at a very reasonable price which will give you 'broadcast quality' results. The Marantz models CP230 and CP430 are the best around for oral history, with the Sony Professional cassette recorder as a second best. Either are suitable for oral history and should ensure good results when used correctly.

Failing these there are many small personal stereo cassette recorders like the Sony or Sanyo 'Walkman' for under £100. Many of this type have built-in microphones which give poor results, so it is best to find one with a socket into which an external microphone can be plugged. This is something to watch out for in any tape recorder. So too are cassette recorders which have what is called a noise reduction system, like Dolby. This reduces the levels of tape hiss during recordings and in the case of DbX prevents what is known as 'print-through', a slight echoey effect. Dolby B is most common but beware of machines which offer Dolby on playback only.

Video recording has the benefit of adding the dimension of moving pictures to interviews. It records not merely the voice but the face, gestures and mannerisms, dress and environment, which can sometimes add to the interest of the recording. It is also possible to include shots of someone at work, demonstrating something, or perhaps walking somewhere significant from childhood.

Video recorders (camcorders) are more expensive than audio recorders and there are several formats to choose from, most of which give good quality results. As with audio recorders it is best to use an external microphone to avoid picking up hum from the camcorder's motor, and because it is sometimes difficult to get close enough to get good sound quality. It is also vital to have a tripod for the camera when interviewing as it will give rock-steady images and enables smooth zooming in and out when filming. It is possible, for example, to start with a wide-shot to put the person in context with their surroundings; move mid-shot (head and shoulders) for most of the interview; and then use close-up (face only) for particularly poignant moments.

Nowadays most portable audio and video tape recorders will run on batteries and using rechargeable batteries saves a lot of money. Some recorders will have built-in rechargeable batteries which can be plugged in to the mains for overnight recharge. It is advisable to avoid using the mains supply when recording as there will sometimes be an annoying hum on the tape picked up from the mains. Using rechargeable batteries also allows recording outside or somewhere remote from mains electricity. It is acceptable to use the mains for playing back your recordings but do not buy a tape recorder which has a mains supply only.

Next in importance to the recorder is a good microphone. For one-to-one interviews indoors tie-clip or lapel microphones are best. There are several makes available, ranging from Tandy's and Maplin's to Sony's. All are relatively cheap. If the tape recorder in use records in stereo and has two microphone sockets, get two microphones — one for your interviewee and one for yourself. They can be attached discreetly to your clothing and give excellent results: however excitable an interviewee the microphone remains close to the action and at an even recording level. In many cases people forget they are wearing them completely and this is an essential part of minimising the technology so you can concentrate on the interview itself. Lapel mikes operate using small 'hearing aid' type batteries and should last over 100 hours in normal use.

For interviews outdoors or on the move it is best to buy a uni-directional hand-held microphone (also known as a cardioid) which will pick up less unwanted noise. They cost slightly more and the best makes to look out for are Beyer, AKG or Sennheiser. Finally, for recording a group of people talking, say around a table, use two uni-directional hand-held microphones and place them back-to-

back on stands. Or, if your recorder has only one microphone socket, there are some cheap flat or 'pressure zone' microphones on the market which give adequate results.

Generally, the more you spend the better the recording equipment you are likely to get. Do not cut corners or you will be disappointed when you come to listening back to the results. However, it is well worth looking out for second-hand or reconditioned tape recorders at reputable dealers, and asking for educational discounts. Alternatively it is sometimes possible to borrow equipment from local groups, local radio station, library or museum. There is also a network of oral history projects all over the country which will sometimes be prepared to lend equipment and provide basic training (a list of some of these groups appears below).

When it comes to tape, Zonal or Ampex standard or long-play tape is recommended for reel-to-reel recorders, recording at a fast speed: either 7.5 or 3.75 inches per second (ips). Cassette recorders all run at the same speed and have the advantage of using cassette tapes which are compact, cheap and easy to load. They have the disadvantage that they cannot be edited without first copying (dubbing) them onto reel-to-reel tape. When buying cassettes, reputable makes are best, like TDK, Agfa, BASF, or Maxell, and use only C60s which last for one hour (thirty minutes per side). Avoid C90s and C120s, which can break or mangle up in your recorder. It is not necessary to buy the more expensive chromium or metal type of cassette: the ordinary ferric (FE) is perfectly adequate for oral history. Sometimes the manufacturer

A member of Bradford's Ukrainian community is interviewed by Ather Khan of the Bradford Heritage Unit.

of your recorder will recommend a particular type of cassette which best suits the machine. It is well worth looking out for special offers on cassettes in shops, and another way of saving money is to buy in bulk direct from manufacturers. Whatever the tape, set the controls on the recorder to match the type of tape. If the original recording was carried our using Dolby B then set the machine to Dolby B when playing it back.

Once all the equipment has been acquired it is a good idea to familiarise yourself with how it all works, so that during the interview you can concentrate wholeheartedly on the interviewee not the machine. Read the instruction book carefully and try doing a mock interview with a friend or relative. This should iron out any technical problems and give you confidence both in using the equipment and in asking questions.

The interview

There are several ways you can approach someone you want to interview, depending on who they are. For many people the best way is initially by letter, followed by a telephone call. A letter establishes your credentials and the seriousness of the project, whilst a phone call gives an opportunity to introduce yourself, explain the project in detail and the aim of the interview, and outline the sort of topics you might cover in your conversation. Invariably you will be asked about what will happen to the tapes afterwards, so this should have been decided in advance. Some people are reassured that it might be going into an archive, others intimidated by this. The person you have approached may also be uncertain at first: they might say they have nothing interesting to say. So you sometimes have to do a bit of persuading. The key is to talk in terms of 'a chat about the past' or a 'story of your life' rather than an interview, which has connotations of officialdom. It is often the more reticent individuals who are the best interviewees.

Use your phone call to get background information and decide where the interview should take place. The person's own home is by far the best as they will be much more relaxed in familiar surroundings. A workplace is an alternative but you are much more likely to be disturbed and distracted. Professional studios give the best technical results but can be officious and uncomfortable places.

It is important to be precise about the arrangements for your visit on the phone and if possible send a follow-up letter setting out the time and date agreed. Any letter sent should be informal: some people are impressed with letterheads but some find them intimidating, particularly those in regular contact with local government bureaucracy, such as social services or the unemployment benefit office. Bear this in mind if, as part of a group, you are designing leaflets and stationery. Your letter and conversation should make it clear that a one-to-one interview is best. Privacy encourages an atmosphere of trust and honesty. A third person present, even a close partner, can inhibit and influence free discussion. Nevertheless there are occasions when a group of people reminiscing together can spark off each other with excellent results. Many local reminiscence groups operate in this way, taking a different conversation topic each week, recording the discussion and writing up the highlights afterwards.

There are mixed feelings among oral historians about whether you should make a preliminary visit to your interviewee before you actually commence recording. While it has the advantage of forging a relationship, there is a danger of losing natural spontaneity when you start to record. Generally you will find a preliminary visit unnecessary. Once the interview has begun it is always possible to go back over ground covered inadequately in the early stages.

Before leaving base test that all the equipment is working properly. Ensure you have enough tape — always take more than you think you will need — and some spare batteries for both the recorder and the microphones. A mains lead is also a good insurance policy if the worst happens.

Arrive promptly and offer some form of identification if the interviewee is unsure about opening the door to you. A shake of the hand and a friendly smile can help break the ice. Once inside remember the whole time that you are their guest and, if they are elderly, that you may be the first person they have spoken to for several days. They will be as nervous and apprehensive as you are, so it is essential to be cordial, reassuring and patient.

Find out where it is that you will be interviewing them. For best results try to pick a room which has lots of soft furnishings and not on a busy road. Respect their favourite chair and sit as close as possible, preferably facing them alongside at a slight angle. Eliminate any extraneous noises like radios, televisions, background noise and clocks. Pets can be a nuisance and budgerigars can be kept quiet by and helps to make the presence of the recorder secondary to developing a relationship with the interviewee. If you are using a clip-on microphone, put it about nine inches from the person's mouth. If you are embarrassed about doing this ask them to do it and make sure the lead is tucked well away under their arm. When using a hand-held microphone on a stand, place it as near to them as possible but not on the same surface as the recorder nor on a hard surface which gives poor sound quality. Generally, the closer the microphone the better the results.

Put yourself and your interviewee at ease by keeping up conversation whilst you are adjusting the recording level controls on your recorder. When you are ready move smoothly into your first question: 'Can you tell me when and where you were born?' Keep all your questions short, clear and to the point. Do not ask too many questions or try to impress by using long words. Your aim is to get them to talk, not to talk yourself. Do not interrupt answers: always wait for a pause. Make sure they can tell you what they think matters most: and never cut them off in mid flow. It is most important that you listen intently and maintain good eye contact. Respond positively and regularly by making appropriate non-verbal signs of encouragement. Body language like nodding and smiling is much better than 'ers' and 'ums' and 'reallys'. It is vital to be relaxed, unhurried and sympathetic. Do not contradict: be tolerant of prejudices.

An interview with a victim of Stalin's repressions assisted by an interpreter.

covering up their cage. Fridges, fires, personal computers and strip-lights can all create a lot of irritating background noise but short of moving to another room there is little you can do. If you are interviewing someone at work ask if they can have their phone and intercom diverted. As you do more interviews you will find you develop an ear for unwanted noise and it is well worth taking time to get the best possible recording.

Set up the equipment so that it is not directly between the two of you, preferably where you can see it but they cannot. This avoids distractions

Try to avoid revealing your own opinions as it can influence what you are told, except in exceptional cases when interviewing on sensitive subjects (for example the Holocaust). In such instances expressions of empathy and reassurance show that the interviewer is human and are likely to lead to greater confidence and openness.

Be ready to follow any interesting avenues. Allow a certain amount of digression, but do not be tempted to switch the recorder off. Go back over anything you were uncertain about and do not be afraid to press for more details, but do not jump from one subject to another too abruptly. Be aware of any inconsistencies and bias in what they say and probe more deeply if you can. As well as a mere descriptive retelling of events, try to explore motives and feelings with questions like 'Why?' and 'How did you feel?' Getting behind stereotype and generalisation is one of the most challenging aspects of oral history. Define dates, names and places as precisely as you can without interrupting the flow of the interview and note down any names to be checked later. Check the recording levels periodically during the interview. When you turn the tape over ask your interviewee to repeat anything interesting you may have missed.

With older people it is important to be sensitive of tiredness and the need for a break. Sometimes you will both be so involved that you may not have noticed time passing. Do not overstay your welcome but equally do not rush away when the interview has finished. Take time to build a closer relationship by talking about yourself and

accepting a cup of tea. You will often be shown some old photographs or documents which add to the oral testimony. Or they will suggest other interesting people you could talk to. With the tape recorder off they will occasionally tell you things they do not want recorded. It is essential that you respect their confidence.

Before you leave thank the interviewee warmly and reassure them that it has been a useful recording. Leave an address or phone number where you can be contacted and make it clear whether you will be returning for a follow-up session or not. This can avert any unnecessary worry. Remember that your visit will often have had a profound impact on someone who has perhaps never told anyone their memories before.

After the interview

Your interview tapes should be treated in the same way you would any other valuable historical document. The original recording should never be edited or interfered with in any way.

The first thing to do after the interview is to mark clearly each cassette or spool (and their boxes) in block capitals with the interviewee's full name, date of birth, date of recording and a unique number, using a permanent black felt tip marker. By keeping a master or accession list of all your interviews each new recording can be given the next number. This enables you to store the tapes in chronological order and find them quickly. Secondly, if you are using cassettes, break the two small safety lugs at the top of the cassette. Once removed it is impossible to erase or over-record your original recording accidentally. Thirdly, write a letter to the interviewee thanking them for their time, reminding them of the project's purpose, and emphasising the value of their tape.

Next, write or type out an interview summary sheet which includes its number; the interviewee's full name; their date of birth; your name and group or organisation; the place and date of the interview; the total number of tapes used; the type of tape recorder used and whether any noise reduction system like Dolby was used; and finally a detailed listed summary of the contents of each tape. Keep a separate list of the interviewees' addresses to protect their confidentiality.

Listening back provides an ideal opportunity to make a copy of each tape, which is highly recommended if you have access to another tape recorder. Many modern domestic hi-fi systems have twin cassette decks which are ideal for this. But if you have not either of these a local oral history project, archive or library will often be willing to help, and may have a cassette duplicator that copies at a fraction of real time. You may want to consider giving them your master tapes for safekeeping in return for a copy which you can use without worry. Replaying and summarising your interview also enables you to assess your own performance and highlight any key areas you missed. What the interviewee said will sometimes take on new meanings and give you new insights not apparent at the time. Finally it is also a chance to make a note of any particularly illuminating stories or striking images for later use.

Careful storage of the tapes is vital: always ensure they are kept upright in their own boxes in shady, cool, dry and dust-free conditions. The best temperature is around 18 degrees centigrade (65 degrees fahrenheit) with a relative humidity of between 40% and 50%. Violent fluctuations of temperature and humidity are particularly to be avoided. Never store tapes in direct sunlight, near a radiator or in a smokey room. Avoid touching the tape itself with your fingers as grease will attract dust and possibly fungal growth. Stray magnetic fields coming from television sets, magnetic door fastenings, transformers and loudspeakers have been known to erase or partially erase tapes, so keep them well away — at least one metre. High voltage cabling has no effect on magnetic tape nor do metal storage cabinets, but lightning conductors are a hazard and tape should be stored at least one metre away. Finally, store your tapes securely where they cannot be interfered with or removed without your knowledge, especially if they are the only copies.[26]

Once numbered, copied and summarised the tapes can be transcribed into written form. This will make each tape quickly accessible to other people who may not have the time to listen to a two or three hour interview. It is a long and laborious process and requires a typewriter or word-processor and a playback machine with headphones and remote control footpedal. This keeps both hands free and saves lots of time by allowing you to pause and rewind the tape easily. Word processors and personal computers are ideal for making and storing transcripts: they can be easily corrected and produce

Interview summary sheet

F1466 Side A

Born 13.12.1910 in Birmingham. Fifth in family of six - two
elder brothers and two elder sisters. JB was 5 and a half
years younger than the fourth child and her sister Mary four
years younger than herself.

Grandparents Only maternal grandmother still alive during
JB's childhood - visited occasionally but JB had little
recollection of her. The other grandparents had died before
JB's birth. Mother's parents had moved to Dublin - hence
infrequency of visits from grandmother.

Parents Father Arthur Wells was a photographer. Mother,
Florence Wells. They had met and married in London - later
moved to Birmingham for her father's business. Lived in
large house on the Moseley Road close to the city centre - a
lot of shops and groups of older houses - lived in one of
these. Remembers a very happy childhood, playing in large
garden with her sister Mary and the boy next door. Also
remembers some resentment because of age gap between she and
Mary and the older siblings - they were always referred to
as "The children". Parents were greatest influence on her
life, particularly her mother. Both were Quakers and JB was
brought up and remained a Quaker until the 1939 war.

Father mainly concerned with his work - mother always at
home. Family always had one maid - the maids were girls
from the Black country who went into "service". Mother
always fed them, as she did the whole family, very well, and
they left looking very well-nourished and were always happy
with the family. JB remembers being very friendly with the
maids and kept in touch with some.

Education Older siblings went to Quaker boarding school
near Banbury. One of the brothers was very ill when away at

So how many of you were taken out?

This I can't tell you. The Polish of us were up to two
hundred, but I don't know if he was collecting from other
blocks or ours as well, but when we got to the working camp
there were two hundred Polish Jewish girls and eight hundred
Hungarian Jewish girls you see. So it was a thousand. When
we got there we dressed ourselves outside the block and then
they took us to a place, we had to strip ourselves again, left
our clothes out behind and there were showers on top. Now
what's going to come out, is it to come out gas or water, we
were all holding ourselves with our hands like that,
(demonstrates). And what is going to be, gas or water. Water
starts coming out and if you can hear everybody, "Thank God".
After we had the bath they didn't shave us anymore. After we
had a bath I don't know how we dried ourselves, you know it's
a funny thing how things are coming to you. But the next
thing I know they were giving us clothes, shoes...

Clean clothes?

They were warm. You see from time to time even in Auschwitz
when I was there, we were disinfected, all the time they were
taking us to have a wash and different dresses. But in the
seams you could see dead lice you see. So you scraped it out
and put it on. But in Auschwitz they only gave us a dress,
which this man gave me clothes, but not knickers you see.
This was the worst time. But still when they were giving us
clothes, they gave us coats, but they all had red crosses.
They gave us dresses, shoes and stockings. I asked her to
give me a towel, so she gave me like a towelling rag, so I
tied it up on both sides as knickers and I also asked her for
something to cover the head, so she gave me a slip, so this I
tore in half and gave Bella my friend, because we were

Sample transcript page

23

Sample copyright and clearance form.

---

multiple copies when required. Desk top publishers can produce very professional results.

The basic rule of transcription is to render the original speech into text as accurately as possible by including repetition, hesitation, exclamation and emphasis, and by reproducing rhythms of speech and dialect words. Never correct the grammar or tidy up what you hear to make it like written language. Each transcript title-page should include the main details from the summary sheet and each page should include its own and the interview number. If you are working as a group it is probably useful to have a house-style sheet so that each transcript is produced in the same way.

Transcribing precisely what is said verbatim can take five to ten minutes for each minute of speech, depending on the quality of the original recording, the clarity of the interview, and whether the interviewee has either an accented voice or uses foreign or technical words. It is an art demanding concentration, accuracy and patience. If you have limited resources it is worth being selective. You could, for example, transcribe a small selection of interviews in full or only short sections of a greater number, depending on how they will be used.[27]

With a summary sheet, and perhaps a transcript, it is now possible to index the recordings. It is useful to keep copies of the summary sheets in both number and name sequence, and you may want to keep a card index system of your interviewees' names for quick reference. A detailed card catalogue or computer index for your tapes can take a long time to develop. Initially, one useful approach is to compile a list of key subject area headings and names from each summary sheet. These can form references to go on alphabetical index cards or into a computer database, and extra entries can be added over time from other interviews. Obviously a system like this is only useful once you have, or are likely to have, very many tapes. It does rely on having the time to do it and on developing a list of agreed subject headings which can standardise your entries.[28]

Ultimately the aim of all this documentation is to make the original material easily usable and readily accessible. However, discretion is the key. Before or after the interview it is important that you explain in detail to the interviewee how you intend to use their taped life story. They may not always be aware that their experiences could be published, sold or broadcast in a variety of ways, and should be offered the chance to restrict access to their interview in any way they wish. Recent changes in copyright law now give the interviewee legal ownership of the copyright in their words, in the same way that an author owns copyright of a book. Although the law allows limited use of copyrighted material under the 'fair dealing' provision of the act, for example quotation for critical reviews and private research study, to avoid infringing copyright it is necessary for the interviewer to ask that copyright be assigned or passed over. You can explain your intentions by letter, but for a public project, or if you intend to deposit your tapes in an archive, this is best done through an access and clearance form, signed by both parties in which the interviewee may agree to assign copyright and thus allow totally free use, restrict the whole interview for a number of years or stipulate that it may not, for instance, be broadcast or used in public talks.[29]

Aside from the ethical argument, a clearance form is an insurance policy in the event of the interviewee's death when something in writing is better than a verbal agreement. They should be clear and uncomplicated, written in plain language. Once completed, copies should be stored with each tape and transcript. If an interview is completely restricted it is a good idea to put it in a sealed envelope or box. At the very least, mark it clearly, perhaps with a permanent red sticky label. It is essential that the interviewees' wishes are respected. As a matter of courtesy consult them before you make any substantial public use of their life stories and above all if this is to include their own name.

Using Oral History

There are many ways in which oral history recordings can be used, the most obvious of which is to publish them in some form. Life story interviews do not fit easily into typical written history. Their strength is in their vividness of personal detail, and their particular turn of phrase; their cumulative indication of feelings and relationships, and their coherence in following one person's life path. Much of this gets lost when interviews are chopped into fragments and interpreted to illustrate an argument. With a little editing, a good interview can often say more as a straightforward document.

But before publishing anything, the essential first step is to assess the quality of the interview: looking for its strengths but also, for example, watching for internal inconsistency, for signs of bias, and making comparisons with evidence from other interviews and documents. As we have seen misremembering can be interesting in itself, but incoherence or vagueness rarely so.

The simplest kind of oral history publication is a single life story. This form gives full expression to someone with an exceptionally fertile memory and particularly interesting life experiences. The transcribed interview is edited — cut and shaped into a coherent narrative — and put into context through an introduction. Some of the most powerful and revealing oral history books have been single spoken autobiographies: such as Raphael Samuel's *East End Underworld* (1981), with its story of urban crime and poverty, or Angela Hewins' *The Dillen* (1981), Stratford-upon-Avon through the eyes of an orphan brought up among its bawds and lodging-house labourers.

A more common type of publication is a collection of oral testimonies. The life stories, or relevant parts of them, are edited and assembled to focus on a particular place or theme. The editor's skill in grouping, juxtaposing and contrasting the material is crucial in giving a collection its shape and its message. Examples include the books of Studs Terkel and Tony Parker, Mary Chamberlain's *Fenwomen: a portrait of women in an English village* (1975), Margot Farnham's *Inventing ourselves: lesbian life stories* (1989), Cahal Dallat and Faith Gibson's *Rooms of time: memories of Ulster people* (1988), Zoe Joseph's *Survivors: Jewish refugees in Birmingham 1933-1945* (1988), and Imran, Smith and Hyslop's *Here to stay: Bradford's South Asian communities* (1994).

An alternative published use of oral history is as one of several sources in a more traditional historical interpretation in which the author sets out to construct an argument, interweaving extracts from interviews with analysis. An example is Jerry White's *Rothschild Buildings: life in an East End tenement block 1887-1920* (1980), a microcosm of London life portraying the changing family, work and culture of three generations of Jewish immigrants. Others include Elizabeth Roberts, *A woman's place: an oral history of working class women 1890-1940* (1984); Steve Humphries, *Hooligans or rebels?: an oral history of working class childhood and youth 1889-1939* (1981); and Alun Howkins, *Poor labouring men: rural radicalism in Norfolk, 1872-1923* (1985). These books succeed partly because they use oral evidence where it is strongest. They focus on hidden, undocumented worlds: family lives, women's lives, village politics. And especially important, they use life stories to make connections which are difficult through other documents.

If you wish to publish but are not used to writing one possibility is to edit together transcribed extracts from a number of interviews on one topic, say school memories, which together could form an oral history narrative. Although large publishers may not be interested, publishing a collection like this in booklet form is not as difficult as it sounds in the days of computerised desk-top publishing. You can often get practical help from your local community arts organisation and they might even give you a small grant to cover costs. An excellent example of this is *The times of our lives: women in Medway from 1900* (Gillingham, 1989), an older women's local history project drawing on the memories of sixty women from the Chatham and Gillingham area, supported and financed by Arts in Medway. Check if you have a local writers' workshop or community publisher: they can give you tremendous support and may already have a publishing programme for autobiographical material. For example the Gatehouse Project in Manchester has produced two important oral history books: *Just lately I realise* (1985), five lives of West Indian migrants; and *Day in day out: memories of North Manchester from women in Monsall Hospital* (1985), a selection from taped interviews with recuperating 70-90 year olds. In Brighton QueenSpark have published *Backyard Brighton: photographs and memories of Brighton in the thirties* (1988) which sold phenomenal numbers locally and has been followed with a sequel, *Backstreet Brighton*. Both accompany old photographs of houses with oral testimony from people who lived in them before they were labelled 'slums' and knocked down.

Obviously if you want to sell your publication you will need to make sure it is well-organised and attractive, especially as there are so many local history publications on the market. Photographs and documents collected from your interviewees can help. So too can a snappy cover and an eye-catching title: *Kiss me while my lips are tacky* by the People's Story Reminiscence Group in Edinburgh is a case in point! If you don't have any photographs, take some yourself or borrow some from your local history library or museum. As part of a group you may find someone who can do line drawings and these can be very effective. Your local newspaper or radio station will often be prepared to

A multicultural schools project.

support your booklet and, if you have the time, local bookshops can be persuaded to stock copies on a sale-or-return basis.

An exhibition is another exciting way of using oral history and one which can reach a lot of people. In recent years social history museums have been in the forefront of local oral history work. Some, like Bradford Museums, have themselves run projects and created major regional sound archives with spin-offs into reminiscence, publishing, educational packs and temporary displays.[30] Others, such as Hull and Beamish, have created major new displays based on oral testimony.[31] Southampton Museums developed a whole new approach to educational outreach and community involvement through oral

history project work;[32] and The People's Story museum in Edinburgh was conceived by local people and centres on their memories.[33] As well as traditional museum venues, oral history exhibitions have appeared in places where people who are not normal museum attenders go: libraries, old people's homes and day centres, churches, schools, and waiting rooms. Shopping centres have proved a great success and in Southampton the oral history project borrowed an entire shop unit free of charge to stage an exhibition about the Southampton Blitz. Attendances smashed all records. In Bradford a touring exhibition about St Lukes, a local hospital which had once been the workhouse and was in the process of being knocked down to make way for a modern building, which was based on interviews with staff past and present, was erected in the canteen and then the local library.

It is not necessary to be a museum professional to put an exhibition together. The main rule is to choose a theme and be clear and well-organised when you put the visual and oral material together. Transcribed extracts from interviews are themselves interesting, if they are kept short and to the point, but generally benefit from illustrations. It is helpful to find strong visual material that directly matches the oral history: it gives the whole exhibition more impact. It is also useful to work out a 'story board' by writing out a mini-version of the exhibition on A4 sheets of paper. This gives you a good overview of the whole exhibition so you can spot breaks in the flow and improvements you could make.

There are many ways of actually assembling an exhibition for a wall or screen. One way is to stick typed-up oral history extracts and photographs onto thick card. Card and mounting board comes in a variety of colours and sizes, and eyelets can be punched in each corner to allow it to be hung or pinned to the wall. You can also arrange to have your oral history extracts sent to a professional typesetter. They can make your text look very smart in a variety of sizes and typefaces and all at a very reasonable price. There are also firms which will heat-seal or encapsulate each board or card in a plastic covering. This keeps the whole exhibition clean and protects it so it can tour a variety of venues without looking too dog-eared.

Something else to consider is a tape of edited highlights from the interviews themselves which gives the exhibition

the extra context of sound. You could then do multiple copies for sale, especially if you have access to a cassette duplicator, and in fact audio publications of oral history interviews are a neglected form of publication. Those that have been produced, like the Imperial War Museum's *The First World War remembered*, Stephen Harrison's *Yorkshire farming memories*, and Birmingham Museum's *The boatman's garden*, about life on the canals, are outstanding. Some of the facilities to copy cassettes might be available at a local museum or library, and they may even be prepared to do a joint publication or exhibition with you or your group. At the least they may be able to offer you exhibition space or the loan of some free-standing boards.

Publicity and presentation are key to any successful exhibition and again local newspapers and radio stations are generally keen to help. Oral history exhibitions are very rewarding and extremely popular, and you will be inundated with interesting potential interviewees and offers of help. They are also great opportunities to get your interviewees together, to meet each other and to involve them in using their memories collectively. The Merseyside Docklands Community History Project found that reunions were a good way of beginning projects as well as completing them: their book *The tapestry makers: life and work in Lee's tapestry works, Birkenhead* (1987) started life as a reunion of ex-employees.

If you have been involved in a school-based oral history project you will quickly be aware of the enormous benefits in terms of building self-confidence, and communication and technical skills. It is a way of bringing history to life and of involving elderly people in school activities. But apart from the actual process of collecting oral history, which fits into key stages one and two of the national curriculum, it can be used as original historical source material in schools. For example *Voices of the Holocaust: a cross-curricular resource pack* (1993), a series of interviews with Jewish Holocaust survivors carried out by the National Sound Archive, would fit into a key stage three study unit 4: 'The twentieth-century world'. On the same topic Ambleside Oral History Group's pack, *The Lake District at War* (1988), combines a teacher's booklet with a sixty minute cassette of eye witness accounts of evacuation, rationing, women at work and conscientious objection, drawn from their archive of over 200 hours of recordings. Bolton Oral History Project's pack, *Growing up in Bolton 1900-1940* (1983) goes even further by including photographs, documents, transcripts, notes, a cassette and a bibliography. In Bradford the Heritage Unit evolved a package on immigration experiences, drawing on interviews with a dozen ethnic groups, comprising a book — *Destination Bradford* (1987) — a touring exhibition of the same name, and a teachers' source book — *Here to stay*.

As an individual or group, putting together packs of oral source material for teachers to use is extremely valuable. This might take the form of a small display or booklet; or a series of work cards; or a cassette tape of edited extracts on a particular theme; or a slide-tape pack bringing together taped highlights and photographs. Find a teacher who is interested to advise you on the sort of subject matter which best matches the syllabus, how it

should be presented and how the pupils could be involved. You may find schools willing to give you materials or loan equipment, sometimes through their local teachers' advisory service which are always keen to develop teaching aids.

Oral history often contrasts well with written material, persuading children that they should weigh up different versions of events before arriving at a final conclusion. It is also ideal for classroom follow-up work like exhibitions and creative writing, and has been successfully used as the basis for theatrical productions and dramatic reconstructions. For example pupils at a school in Vauxhall in south London based a play — 'Motherland' — on their mothers' experiences of coming to Britain from the West Indies,[34] and since then Age Exchange Theatre Company have been one of a number of locally-based groups all over Britain which have performed pieces of theatre derived from interviews with older people. In Age Exchange's case this has evolved into the setting up of a reminiscence centre running reminiscence workshops for professional carers, and in lavishly produced booklets. Latterly they have become involved in youth theatre and in role play with children in recreated Edwardian classrooms and as evacuees.[35] In this way the oral testimonies are used as the basis for a 'realistic recreation' in which the children actually 'live in the past'.

Creating a slide-tape programme is one way of making use of oral history with older people. A slide show of local photographs added to hearing the voices of other people recalling the past can be very entertaining and evocative, especially if the tape

Oral history brings generations together.

includes some old songs. It will encourage reminiscence, which is often in itself beneficial to older people and can yield new and useful information. It can also persuade them to write down or record their own life experiences. Old people's homes, clubs and day centres welcome a slide show or talk about the past. It is a great opportunity to try out what you have collected as they will give you a tremendous feedback. An initial talk can lead on to a more regular reminiscence session, sometimes through a care assistant or adult education tutor. Or you may want to start a group yourself.

Reminiscence work is increasingly popular in old people's homes, sheltered accommodation, hospitals and social work, and a range of guides and resources have emerged since Help the Aged's innovative *Recall* slide-tape packs in 1981. There is still some debate amongst professional carers and gerontologists about whether reminiscence has a therapeutic effect or not.[36] Results have been mixed and one of the difficulties has been the shortage of good locally-produced stimulus materials. Some oral history projects have stepped in. Dundee Oral History Project, for example, produced an excellent *Guide to reminiscence* (1986) as well as a series of packs on topics like school life and streetlife; and Gatehouse in Manchester put together *Then and now: a training pack for reminiscence work* (1992). Historians and carers are beginning to work together all over Britain in one of the most positive and community relevant roles for history for many years.

Producing a slide-tape pack is not as daunting as it sounds. When copying photographs or documents onto slides, put them flat under some glass, light them well, and re-photograph them onto black and white slide film. One way of rough editing a tape together is by copying the chosen extracts from the master tape onto another tape. This can be done with cassette tape, but to get a more finished product you will need to copy onto an open reel tape, then edit it using an editing block, a sharp blade and splicing tape. You can buy tape editing kits quite cheaply. Or there are now some computer software programmes which enable sound editing on a personal computer keyboard.[37]

Local radio stations are always keen to feature local history. Oral history is ideal, especially if the quality of the original recording is good. Apart from actually using your own recordings it is also a chance to publicise your work or group, and attract more potential interviewees. There will sometimes be look-back programmes which you could offer an item for, or phone-ins on a particular topic. Talking newspapers and magazines for the blind and disabled are another outlet for your tapes and an important way of encouraging disabled people to record their own stories. Yorkshire Art Circus, for example, published an account from six people of their experiences of spinal injury, *Looking up* (1989); and in the same part of the country important work has been done with the mentally ill.[38]

There are now many local history libraries and archives around the country geared up for safeguarding oral history tapes and making them

publicly accessible. Increasing numbers are recognising the value of oral testimony in making up deficiencies in their coverage of the past through their book collection. They may be frequently unable to answer public enquiries about, for example, the history of local ethnic groups or industry, and a collection of oral history tapes could plug the gaps. Oral history can also assist in interpreting other documentary archive material more accurately. It is a good idea to arrange to deposit your master tapes, or at least copies, with one of these as soon as you can. Make sure you also include as much documentation as you can. They will sometimes have funds to produce cassette and transcript copies, and will possibly be interested in a series of edited highlight cassettes for loan which could introduce users to the wider collection. If local deposit is not possible or you think you have a recording which is of national interest, then you should contact the curator of oral history at the National Sound Archive. The NSA can often house material and give more general advice on the correct storage and archiving conditions for oral history tapes.

Oral history is thought-provoking, challenging, exciting to collect, rewarding to use and historically vitally important if we are to have not only a more accurate picture of our past, but also a more rounded view, which takes full account of society's marginalised groups as well as those with influence. Oral history reminds us that history is made up of individuals with unique experiences and infinitely different ways of living their lives.

Notes and References

1   *Elizabeth Roberts*, **A woman's place: an oral history of working class women 1890-1940**, Oxford: Blackwell, 1984, p.73.

2   NSA City Lives interview C409/27. See also *Anthony Seldon* and *Joanna Pappworth*, **By word of mouth: 'elite' oral history**, Methuen, 1983.

3   *Tim Edensor* and *Mij Kelly* (eds.), **Moving worlds: personal recollections of twenty-one immigrants to Edinburgh**, Edinburgh: Polygon, p.151.

4   Bradford Heritage Recording Unit interview B0166, available at Bradford Central Library.

5   *Raphael Samuel*, **East End Underworld: chapters in the life of Arthur Harding**, Routledge, 1981, pp.75-6.

6   See *Paul Thompson*, **The voice of the past: oral history**, Oxford, OUP, second edition 1988; *Raphael Samuel* and *Paul Thompson* (eds.), **The myths we live by**, Routledge, 1990.

7   *Alex Haley*, **Roots**, Hutchinson, 1977.

8   From the 1955 *L. Shirley-Price* translation, p.34.

9   **Oral History**, vol.1, no.3, p.46

10 Quoted in *Paul Thompson*, **The voice of the past**, p.30.

11 The first volume appeared in 1889 followed by seventeen in all by 1903.

12 Reprinted by Virago in 1979. *Mary Chamberlain's* **Growing up in Lambeth,** Virago, 1989, is an attempt to update the original survey using oral history techniques.

13 Three volumes, Macmillan, 1903.

14 **Economic Journal**, vol.xvi, p.522.

15 *Ann Banks*, **First person America**, New York, Random House, 1980; *Eugene Genovese's* **Roll, Jordan, roll: the world the slaves made**, Deutsch, 1975; and *Theda Perdue's* **Nations remembered: an oral history of five civilized tribes 1865-1907**, Greenwood, 1980, are examples of books based on the New Deal collection.

16 *Allan Nevins*, 'Oral history: how and why it was born', **Wilson Library Bulletin**, no.40 (March 1966), pp.600-1.

17 *Paul Thompson*, **The Edwardians: the remaking of British society**, Weidenfeld and Nicolson, 1975; second edition, Routledge, 1992.

18 See *Sallie Purkis*, **Oral history in schools**, Colchester, Oral History Society, 1981, and 'An experiment in family history with

first year juniors', **Teaching History**, vol.4, no.15 (May 1977); also *Allan Redfern*, **Talking in class: oral history and the national curriculum**, Oral History Society, 1995.

19 *George Ewart Evans*, **Ask the fellows who cut the hay,** Faber, 1956, pp.49-50. See also *Alun Howkins*, 'Inventing everyman: George Ewart Evans, oral history and national identity', **Oral History**, vol.22, no.2 (1994), pp.26-32.

20 *Paul Thompson* and *Joanna Bornat*, 'Interview with Stephen Peet', **Oral History**, vol.10, no.1 (1982), pp.47-55

21 Joanna Bornat, 'Oral history as a social movement: reminiscence and older people', **Oral History**, vol.17, no.2 (1989), pp.16-25 is an excellent overview of this development.

22 See the special issue of **Oral History** devoted to museums and oral history: vol.14, no.2 (1986).

23 Department of Education and Science, **History in the National Curriculum** *(England)*, HMSO, 1991, and its most recent form, Department for Education, **The National Curriculum**, HMSO, 1995. See also the special issue of **Oral History** devoted to the national curriculum: vol.20, no.1 (1992).

24 For a full discussion of memory and oral history see *Thompson*, **Voice of the Past**, second edition, chap.5; *Karen Fields*, 'What one cannot remember mistakenly', **Oral History**, vol.17, no.1 (1989), pp.44-53;

Diane T. Hyland and *Adele Ackerman*, 'Reminiscence and autobiographical memory in the study of the personal past', **Journal of Gerontology**, vol.43, no.2 (1988), pp.35-9; *Alessandro Portelli*, 'Uchronic dreams: working class memory and possible worlds', **Oral History**, vol.16, no.2 (1988), pp.46-56; *Robert Perks*, 'Ukraine's forbidden history: memory and nationalism', **Oral History**, vol.21, no.1 (1993); *Alistair Thomson, Michael Frisch* and *Paula Hamilton*, 'The memory and history debates: some international perspectives', **Oral History**, vol.22, no.2 (1994).

25 See *Paul Thompson* with *Doc Rowe*, 'Ten inches into six feet: low budget equipment for an oral history project', **Oral History**, vol.16, no.1 (1988), pp.55-60, and Paul Thompson with Peter Copeland, 'Why DAT matters to oral historians', **Oral History**, vol.17, no.1 (1989), pp.56-61, which was updated by *Peter Copeland*, 'Technical notes', **Oral History**, vol.20, no.2 (1992).

26 *Alan Ward's* **Manual of sound archive administration**, Gower, 1990, includes much useful information about storage arrangements. *David Lance's* **An archive approach to oral history**, IASA, 1978, is based on the experience of setting up the Department of Sound Records at the Imperial War Museum, and is still excellent.

27 *Mary Jo Deering* and *Barbara Pomeroy*, **Transcribing without tears: a guide to transcribing**

and editing oral history interviews, Washington DC: George Washington University, 1976; *Raphael Samuel*, 'Perils of the transcript', **Oral History**, vol.1, no.2 (1971), pp.19-22.

28 Very little has been published on the special problems of indexing and cataloguing oral history recordings but see *Jim Fitzpatrick* and *Stuart Reid*, 'Indexing a large scale oral history project', **Oral History**, vol.15, no.1 (1987), pp.54-7; *Cathryn Gallacher* and *Dale Treleven*, 'Developing an online database and printed directory and subject guide to oral history collections', **Oral History Review** [US], vol.16, no.1 (Spring 1988), pp.33-68; *Shirley Stephenson*, **Editing and indexing: guidelines for oral history**, Fullerton, Calif.: California State University, 1983.

29 The best understandable guide to recent copyright law and oral history is *Alan Ward's* **Manual**, chap.3. See also *Peter Copeland*, 'Notes on the Copyright, Designs and Patents Act 1988', **BASC News**, no.4 (1989), and the Oral History Society's **Copyright, ethics and oral history** (1995) which includes the Society's ethical guidelines.

30 *Robert Perks*, 'Immigration to Bradford: the oral testimony', **Immigrants and Minorities**, vol.6, no.3 (1987), pp.362-8; 'Using sound archives: Bradford Heritage Unit's oral history collection', **BASC News**, no.2 (1987); Olive Howarth, **Textile voices: mill life this century**, Bradford: BHRU/Bradford Libraries and Information Service, 1989.

31 See *Elizabeth Frostick's* articles, 'The use of oral evidence in the reconstruction of dental history **at Beamish Museum'**, **Oral History**, vol.14, no.2 (1986), pp.59-65; 'Worth a Hull lot more', **Museums Journal**, vol.91, no.2 (1991), pp.33-5.

32 *Sian Jones* and *Carl Major*, 'Reaching the public: oral history as a survival strategy for museums', **Oral History**, vol.14, no.2 (1986), pp.31-8; Southampton Museums Oral History Section, **Woolston before the bridge**, Southampton: Southampton Local Studies Section, 1989.

33 *Helen Clark, Antonia Ineson, Ginnie Moreton* and *Judith Sim*, 'Oral history and reminiscence in Lothian', **Oral History**, vol.17, no.2 (1989), pp.35-42. *Stuart Davies'* article 'Falling on deaf ears? Oral history and strategy in museums', **Oral History**, vol.22, no.2 (1994), is a good overview.

34 *Elyse Dodgson*, **Motherland: West Indian women to Britain in the 1950s**, Heinemann, 1984.

35 Age Exchange have produced many books, including: **A place to stay: memories of pensioners from many lands** (1984), **What did you do in the war, Mum?** (1985), **Can we afford the doctor?** (1985), and **Goodnight children everywhere. Memories of evacuation in World War II** (1990). Also worth reading is *Angela Hewins* 'The RSC's production of "The Dillen"', **Oral History**, vol.12, no.2 (1984), pp.32-7; and Gordon Langley and Baz Kershaw (eds.),

'Reminiscence theatre', **Theatre Papers**, fourth series (1981-2), no.6, based on experimental theatre in the Exeter area.

36 Amongst an enormous literature see: *Joanna Bornat* (ed.), **Reminiscence Reviewed: perspectives, evaluations, achievements**, Buckingham: Open University Press, 1994; *Peter Coleman*, **Ageing and reminiscence processes: social and clinical implications,** Colchester: *John Wiley*, 1986; *Andrew Norris*, **Reminiscence with elderly people**, Winslow, 1986; *John Adams*, 'Reminiscence in the geriatric ward: an undervalued resource', **Oral History**, vol.12, no.2 (1984), pp.54-9; *Susan Thornton* and *Janet Brotchie*, 'Reminiscence: a critical review of the empirical literature', **British Journal of Clinical Psychology**, vol.26 (1987), pp.93-111.

37 *Tim Smith* and *Rob Wilkinson*, 'Setting up a local recall pack', **Oral History**, vol.17, no.2 (1989), pp.43-8.

38 *Rebecca Fido* and *Maggie Potts*, '"It's not true what was written down": experiences of life in a mental handicap institution', **Oral History**, vol.17, no.2 (1989), pp.31-4; Steve Humphries and Pamela Gordon, **Out of sight: the experience of disability 1900-1950**, Plymouth: Northcote House, 1992; *Jan Walmsley*, 'Life history interviews with people with learning disabilities', **Oral History**, vol.23, no.1 (1995).

Further Reading

NB Place of publication London unless otherwise specified.

Introductory books about oral history

George Ewart Evans, **Spoken history**, Faber, 1987.
A conspectus of Evans's pioneering oral history work.

Steve Humphries, **The handbook of oral history: recording life stories**, Inter-action, 1984.
A clear and practical handbook on how to set up an oral history project, especially useful for community work.

Trevor Lummis, **Listening to history: the authenticity of oral evidence**, Hutchinson, 1987.
Focusses on analysing oral history, including quantification.

Anthony Seldon and *Joanna Pappworth*, **By word of mouth: elite oral history**, Methuen, 1983.
Using oral history research methods with elites.

Paul Thompson, **The voice of the past: oral history**, Oxford: Oxford University Press, second edition, 1988.
An essential guide combining an historiographical overview with practical advice, including model questions and a bibliography.

Valerie Raleigh Yow, **Recording oral history: a practical guide for social scientists**, Sage, 1994.
A well-written and accessible guide based on solid experience in the field.

Reference books and readers about oral history:

David Dunaway and *Willa Baum*, **Oral history: an interdisciplinary anthology**, Nashville: American Association for State and Local History/Oral History Association, 1987.

Ruth Finnegan, **Oral traditions and the verbal arts: a guide to research practices**, Routledge, 1992.

Michael Frisch, **A shared authority: essays on the craft and meaning of oral and public history**, New York: University of New York Press, 1990.
A thought-provoking collection from one of the States' foremost oral historians.

Sherna Berger Gluck and *Daphne Patai* (eds.), **Women's words: the feminist practice of oral history**, Routledge, 1991.
Thirteen chapters discussing the ethical and practical issues involved.

Robert Perks, **Oral history: an annotated bibliography**, British Library National Sound Archive, 1990.
The only comprehensive bibliography of oral history in Britain, containing over 2100 entries covering books, articles, periodicals and recordings. It has a subject index to aid fast access.

Robert Perks and *Alistair Thomson*, **Oral history reader**, Routledge, 1996.
A broad-ranging international anthology.

David Trask and *Robert Pomeroy*, **The craft of public history: an annotated select bibliography**, Greenwood, 1983.

Lali Weerasinghe (ed.), **Directory of recorded sound collections in the United Kingdom**, British Library National Sound Archive, 1989.
It lists nearly 500 private and public sound collections — many of them containing oral history — including their addresses, access details and contents.

Archiving oral history

Ken Howarth, **Remember, remember: tape recording oral history**, Pennine Heritage, 1984.
A good short guide to interviewing and archiving.

David Lance, **An archive approach to oral history**, International Association of Sound Archives, 1978.
Excellent on the archiving and documentation of oral history.

William Moss and *Peter Mazikana*, **Archives, oral history and oral tradition: a RAMP study**, Paris: UNESCO, 1986.
A free guide to archival practice drawing on experience from all over the world.

Alan Ward, **Manual of sound archive administration**, Gower, 1990.
The best up-to-date all-round guide, which takes in storage, copyright and conservation.

Oral history and education

Stuart Archer and *Nigel Shepley*, **Witnessing history: looking at oral evidence**, Cheltenham: Thornes, 1988.

Julia Bush, **Moving on: Northamptonshire and the wider world**, Northampton: Nene College, 1989.
A multi-cultural resource pack comprising a book, a video, photographs, documents, transcripts and a teacher's guide.

Alan Dein and *Rob Perks*, **Lives in steel,** British Library, 1993.
A compact disc and cassette of edited extracts from interviews with steelworkers.

Elyse Dodgson, **Motherland: West Indian women to Britain in the 1950s**, Heinemann, 1984.
An educational sourcebook used as the basis for youth drama.

Kirklees Sound Archive, **Transport: a National Curriculum resource pack**, Huddersfield: Kirklees Sound Archive, 1991.

Sallie Purkis, **Oral history in schools**, Oral History Society, 1981.
A good overview for setting up and using oral history in schools, now out-of-print.

Allan Redfern, **Talking in class: oral history and the national curriculum**, Oral History Society, 1995.
A standard work on oral history in schools at all ages.

Elizabeth Roberts, **Voices from the past 1890-1940: an oral history resource for schools**, Lancaster: Centre for North West Regional Studies, 1984.

Pam Schweitzer, **Age exchanges: reminiscence projects for children and older people**, Age Exchange, 1993.

Thad Sitton, George Mehaffy and O.L. Davis, **Oral history: a guide for teachers**, Austin: University of Texas, 1983.
One of the best U.S. manuals for school oral history.

Carrie Supple and Rob Perks, **Voices of the Holocaust: a cross-curricular resource pack**, British Library, 1993.
Four audio cassettes and 72 page book drawn from over 150 interviews with Jewish Holocaust survivors.

Oral history and reminiscence

Joanna Bornat (ed.), **Reminiscence reviewed: perspectives, evaluations, achievements**, Buckingham: Open University Press, 1994.
The best review of reminiscence work in the health and social services fields.

Joanna Bornat, 'Oral history as a social movement: reminiscence and older people', **Oral History**, vol.17, no.2 (1989), pp.16-25.

Peter Coleman, **Ageing and reminiscence processes: social and clinical implications**, Colchester: John Wiley, 1986.

Faith Gibson, **Using reminiscence: a training pack**, Help the Aged, 1989.
A valuable pack comprising a tape-slide programme, a video and manual.

Faith Gibson, **Reminiscence and recall: a guide to good practice**, Age Concern England, 1994.

M. Kaminsky (ed.), **The uses of reminiscence: new ways of working with older adults**, New York: Haworth, 1984.

Jane Lawrence and Jane Mace, **Remembering in groups: ideas from reminiscence and literacy work**, Oral History Society, 1987.

Andrew Norris, **Reminiscence with elderly people**, Winslow Press, 1986.
A brief, if expensive, practical introduction to reminiscence therapy.

Caroline Osborn, **The reminiscence handbook: ideas for creative activities with older people**, Age Exchange, 1993.

Susan Thornton and Janet Brotchie, 'Reminiscence: a critical view of the empirical literature', **British Journal of Clinical Psychology**, vol.26 (1987), pp.93-111.

Publications using oral history

Caroline Adams, **Across seven seas and thirteen rivers: life stories of pioneer Sylhetti settlers in Britain**, THAP, 1987.

Melvyn Bragg, **Speak for England: an essay on England 1900-1975 based on interviews with inhabitants of Wigton, Cumberland**, Secker and Warburg, 1976.

Brighton Ourstory Project, **Daring hearts: lesbian and gay lives of 50s and 60s Brighton**, Brighton: QueenSpark Books, 1992.

Mary Chamberlain, **Fenwomen: a portrait of women in an English village**, Quartet, 1975.

Carl Chinn, **They worked all their lives: women of the urban poor in England, 1880-1939**, Manchester: Manchester University Press, 1988.

Nigel Cross and Rhiannon Barker (eds.), **At the desert's edge: oral** histories from the Sahel, Panos, 1991.

George Ewart Evans, **Where beards wag all: the relevance of the oral tradition**, Faber and Faber, 1970.

George Ewart Evans, **The crooked scythe: an anthology of oral history**, Faber and Faber, 1993.

Ronald Fraser, **Blood of Spain: the experience of civil war 1936-9**, Allen Lane, 1979.

Ronald Fraser, **In search of a past: the Manor House, Amnersfield, 1933-1945**, Verso, 1984.

Eugene Genovese, **Roll, Jordan, roll: the world the slaves made**, Deutsch, 1975.

Nigel Gray, **The worst of times: an oral history of the Great Depression in Britain**, Wildwood, 1985.

Tamara Hareven, **Family time and industrial time: the relationship between the family and work in a New England industrial community**, Cambridge: Cambridge University Press, 1982.

Angela Hewins, **The Dillen: memories of a man of Stratford-upon-Avon**, Oxford: Oxford University Press, 1982.

William Hinton, **Shenfan: the continuing revolution in a Chinese village**, Secker and Warburg, 1983.

Anna Horsbrugh-Porter (ed.), **Memories of revolution: Russian women remember**, Routledge, 1993.

Steve Humphries, **Hooligans or rebels?: an oral history of working class childhood and youth 1889-1939**, Oxford: Blackwell, 1981.

Steve Humphries, **A secret world of sex. Forbidden fruit: the British experience 1900-1950**, Sidgwick and Jackson, 1988.

Steve Humphries, Joanna Mack and Robert Perks, **A century of childhood**, Sidgwick and Jackson, 1988.

Billy Kay (ed.), **Odyssey: Voices from Scotland's recent past**, two volumes, Edinburgh: Polygon, 1980/1982.

Mij Kelly and Tim Edensor, **Moving worlds**, Edinburgh: Polygon, 1989

Jill Liddington and Jill Norris, **One hand tied behind us: the rise of the women's suffrage movement**, Virago, 1978.

Mary Loudon, **Unveiled: nuns talking**, Chatto and Windus, 1992.

Lyn Macdonald, **The roses of no man's land**, Michael Joseph, 1980.

Lyn Macdonald, **Somme**, Michael Joseph, 1983.

Betty Messenger, **Picking up the linen threads: a study in industrial folklore**, Belfast: Blackstaff, 1980.

Ronnie Munck and Bill Rolston with Gerry Moore, **Belfast in the thirties: an oral history**, Belfast: Blackstaff, 1987.

Tony Parker, **The people of Providence: a housing estate and some of its inhabitants**, Hutchinson, 1983.

Tony Parker, **Soldier, soldier**, Heinemann, 1985.

Tony Parker, **Russian voices**, Jonathan Cape, 1991.

Tony Parker, **May the Lord in his mercy be kind to Belfast**, Jonathan Cape, 1993.

Luisa Passerini, **Fascism in popular memory**, Cambridge: Cambridge University Press, 1987.

Luisa Passerini (ed.), **International Yearbook of Oral History and Life Stories. Volume 1: memory and totalitarianism**, Oxford: Oxford University Press, 1993.

Ken Plummer, **Documents of life: an introduction to the problems and literature of a humanistic method**, Allen Unwin, 1983.

Alessandro Portelli, **The death of Luigi Trastulli and other stories: form and meaning in oral history**, Albany: SUNY Press, 1991.

Maggie Potts and *Rebecca Fido*, **'A fit person to be removed'. Personal accounts of life in a mental deficiency institution**, Plymouth: Northcote House, 1991.

Elizabeth Roberts, **A woman's place: an oral history of working class women 1890-1940**, Oxford: Blackwell, 1984.

Elizabeth Roberts, **Women and families: an oral history, 1940-70**, Oxford: Blackwell, 1995.

Raphael Samuel, **East End underworld: chapters in the life of Arthur Harding**, Routledge, 1981.

Raphael Samuel and *Paul Thompson*, **The myths we live by**, Routledge, 1990.

Hugo Slim and *Paul Thompson* (eds.), **Listening for change: oral testimony and development**, Panos, 1993.

Joe Smith, **Off the record: an oral history of pop music**, Sidgwick and Jackson, 1989.

Studs Terkel, **Division Street, America**, Penguin, 1970.

Studs Terkel, **Working**, New York: Wildwood, 1974; Penguin, 1985.

Studs Terkel, **'The Good War': an oral history of World War Two**, Hamilton, 1985.

Paul Thompson, **The Edwardians: the remaking of British society**, Wiedenfeld and Nicolson, 1975; second edition, Routledge, 1992.

Paul Thompson and *Natasha Burchardt* (eds.), **Our common history: the transformation of Europe**, Pluto, 1982.

Paul Thompson with *Tony Wailey* and *Trevor Lummis*, **Living the fishing**, Routledge, 1983.

Thea Thompson, **Edwardian childhoods**, Routledge, 1981.

Alistair Thomson, **Anzac memories: living with the legend**, Oxford University Press, 1994.

Elizabeth Tonkin, **Narrating our pasts: the social construction of oral history**, Cambridge: Cambridge University Press, 1992.

Jerry White, **Rothschild buildings: life in an East End tenement block 1887-1920**, Routledge, 1980.

Jerry White, **The worst street in North London: Campbell Bunk, Islington, between the wars**, Routledge, 1986.

Eliot Wigginton (ed.), **The Foxfire Books**, New York: Doubleday, nine vols. 1972-86

Amrit Wilson, **Finding a voice: Asian women in Britain**, Virago, 1978.

Xinxin Zhang and *Sang Ye*, **Chinese lives**, Penguin, 1989.

Useful Contacts

National:

British Library National Sound Archive/National Life Story Collection, c/o Curator of Oral History, 29 Exhibition Road, London SW7 2AS. Tel: 0171-412-7405/7404.

Oral History Society and Journal, c/o Department of Sociology, University of Essex, Wivenhoe Park, Colchester, CO4 3SQ. Tel: 01206-873333.

Imperial War Museum, Department of Sound Records, Lambeth Road, London SE1 6HZ. Tel: 0171-416-5000.

Federation of Worker Writers and Community Publishers (FWWCP), PO Box 540 Burslem, Stoke-on-Trent ST6 6DR. Tel: 01782-822327.

Mass Observation Archive, The Library, Sussex University, Falmer, Brighton BN2 9QL. Tel: 01273-678157.

National Register of Archives, Quality House, Quality Court, Chancery Lane, London WC2A 1HP. Tel: 0171-242-1198.

British Council of Organisations of Disabled People, De Bradlei House, Chapel Street, Belper, Derbyshire DE5 1AR. Tel: 01773-828182, Minicom: 828195.

Selected Regional Contacts:

London:

Museum of London, London Wall, London EC2Y 5HN. Tel: 0171-600-3699

Age Exchange Reminiscence Centre, 11 Blackheath Village, London SE3 9LA. Tel: 0181-318-9105

Ethnic Communities Oral History Project, Hammersmith and Fulham Urban Studies Centre, The Lilla Huset, 191 Talgarth Road, London W6 8BJ. Tel: 0181-741-7138.

Island History Trust, Island House, Roserton Street, London E14 3PG. Tel: 0171-987-6041.

Kensington and Chelsea Community History Group, 1 Thorpe Close, London W10 5XL. Tel: 0181-968-0921.

South:

Dorset Sound Archive, Dorset County Record Office, Bridport Road, Dorchester, Dorset DT1 1RP. Tel: 01305-250550.

Southampton City Heritage Oral History Section, Tower House, Town

Quay, Southampton SO1 1DX.
Tel: 01703-635904.

Oral History Department, Royal Naval Museum, HM Naval Base, Portsmouth, Hampshire PO1 3NU.
Tel: 01705-733060.

Wessex Sound and Video Archive, Hampshire Record Office, Sussex Street, Winchester SO23 8TH.
Tel: 01962-847742/846154.

South West:

Beaford Centre and Archive, Greenwarren House, Beaford, Winkleigh EX19 8LU. Tel: 018053-201.

Dartington Rural Archive, Dartington Hall, Totnes, TQ9 6JE.
Tel: 01803-862224.

East Anglia:

The Essex Sound Archive, Essex Record Office, County Hall, Chelmsford CM1 1LX.
Tel: 01245-492211.

Suffolk Record Office, St.Andrew House, County Hall, St.Helens Street, Ipswich IP4 2JS. Tel: 01473-230000.

Midlands:

Nottingham County Library, Local Studies Section, Angel Row, Nottingham NG1 6HP.
Tel: 0115-941-2412.

Walsall Local History Centre, Essex Street, Walsall WS2 7AS.
Tel: 01922-721305.

City Sound Archive, Social History Department, Birmingham Museum of Science and Industry, Newhall Street, Birmingham B3 1RZ.
Tel: 0121-235-1672.

Leicester Living History Unit, Leisure Services, New Walk Centre, Welford Place, Leicester LE1 6ZG.
Tel: 0116-252-7334.

Centre for Oxfordshire Studies, Central Library, Westgate, Oxford OX1 1DJ.
Tel: 01865-815432.

The Living Archive Project, The Old Bath House, 205 Stratford Road, Wolverton, Milton Keynes MK12 5RL.
Tel: 01908-322568.

Welsh Borders:

Shropshire County Museum Service, Wenlock Lodge, Acton Scott, Church Stretton SY6 6QN. Tel: 016946-306.

Yorkshire:

Centre for English Cultural Tradition and Language, University of Sheffield, Sheffield S10 2TN.
Tel: 0114-276-8555.

Yorkshire Art Circus, School Lane, Glasshoughton, Castleford WF10 4QH.
Tel: 01977-603028.

Bradford Heritage Recording Unit, Industrial Museum, Moorside Road, Bradford BD2 3HP.
Tel: 01274-631756.

Kirklees Sound Archive, Tolson Memorial Museum, Ravensknowle Park, Wakefield Road, Huddersfield HD5 8DJ. Tel: 01484-530591.

Local History Unit, Park Street Centre, Hull College, Park Street, Hull HU2 8RR. Tel: 01482-329943.

North West:

North West Sound Archive, Clitheroe Castle, Clitheroe, Lancashire BB7 1AZ. Tel: 01200-27897.

Centre for North West Regional Studies, University of Lancaster, Bailrigg, Lancaster LA1 4YH. Tel: 01524-65201.

Cumbria:

Ambleside Oral History Group, c/o Ambleside Library, Kelsick Road, Ambleside LA22 0BZ. Tel: 01966-32507.

Scotland:

School of Scottish Studies/Scottish Oral History Group, University of Edinburgh, 27 George Square, Edinburgh EH8 9LD. Tel: 0131-650-1000

People's Story, Canongate Tollbooth, 163 Canongate, Edinburgh EH8 8BN. Tel: 0131-225-2424.

Orkney Sound Archive, Orkney Library, Laing Street, Kirkwall, Orkney. Tel: 01856-3166.

Shetland Archives History Project, c/o County Archives, King Harald Street, Lerwick. Tel: 01595-3535.

Ayrshire Sound Archive Committee, c/o Strathclyde Regional Archives, Mitchell Library, North Street, Glasgow. Tel: 0141-221-7030.

People's Palace, Glasgow Green, Glasgow. Tel: 0141-554-0223.

Wales:

Gwynedd Archives Service, County Offices, Shirehall Street, Caernarfon, Gwynedd LL55 1SH. Tel: 01286-4121.

Welsh Folk Museum, St Fagan's, Cardiff, South Glamorgan CF5 6XB. Tel: 01222-569441.

Clwyd Library and Museum Services, Civic Centre, Mold, Clwyd CH7 6NW. Tel: 01352-2121.

Northern Ireland:

Ulster Society for Oral History, c/o Department and Information Studies, Queens University, University Road, Belfast BT7 1NN. Tel: 01232-245133.

Ulster Folk and Transport Museum, Cultra Manor, Holywood, County Down BT18 0EU. Tel: 01232-428428.